WHALES
OF THE ARCTIC

SARA SWAN MILLER

PowerKiDS
press™
New York

Published in 2009 by The Rosen Publishing Group, Inc.
29 East 21st Street, New York, NY 10010

First Edition

Editor: Amelie von Zumbusch
Book Design: Kate Laczynski
Photo Researcher: Jessica Gerweck

Photo Credits: Back cover (caribou) © www.istockphoto.com/Paul Loewen; back cover (emperor penguins) © www.istockphoto.com/Bernard Breton; back cover (polar bears) © www.istockphoto.com/Michel de Nijs; back cover (seals), pp. 6, 12 Shutterstock.com; back cover (walruses) © Sue Flood/Getty Images; back cover (whales), Cover, pp. 1, 4, 14 © Paul Nicklen/Getty Images; pp. 8, 10, 18 © Flip Nicklen/Getty Images; p. 16 © www.istockphoto.com/Brett Atkins; p. 20 © Gilbert Pajot/Getty Images.

Library of Congress Cataloging-in-Publication Data

Miller, Sara Swan.
  Whales of the Arctic / Sara Swan Miller. — 1st ed.
     p. cm. — (Brrr! Polar animals)
  Includes index.
  ISBN 978-1-4358-2743-1 (library binding) — ISBN 978-1-4358-3147-6 (pbk).
ISBN 978-1-4358-3153-7 (6-pack)
  1. Whale—Arctic regions—Juvenile literature. I. Title.
  QL737.C4M653 2009
  599.5—dc22
                                    2008028748

Manufactured in the United States of America

CONTENTS

WHAT IS A WHALE? 5

AT HOME IN THE SEA 7

A WHALE'S LIFE 9

DEEP-DIVING BOWHEAD WHALES 11

BEAUTIFUL BELUGA WHALES....................................13

STRANGE-LOOKING NARWHALS 15

SINGING HUMPBACK WHALES..................................17

GRAY WHALES ON THE MOVE 19

WHALES AND PEOPLE 21

SAVING THE WHALES 22

GLOSSARY 23

INDEX..24

WEB SITES..24

4

Male narwhals, like these whales, have long, twisting tusks. A tusk is a very long tooth. A small number of female narwhals have tusks, as well.

WHAT IS A WHALE?

People once believed whales were fish! Now we know that they are mammals. Like other mammals, whales are **warm blooded** and drink their mothers' milk as babies. Since they are mammals, whales need to breathe air. Whales come to the **surface** and breathe through blowholes on the tops of their heads.

Whales live all around the world. Many of these huge mammals spend at least part of their time in the Arctic. The Arctic is the area around the North Pole. Some kinds of whales even live year-round in these icy waters. Narwhals, belugas, and bowhead whales all call the Arctic home.

Toothed whales, such as belugas, use their teeth to catch and hold food. These whales swallow their food whole, instead of chewing it.

AT HOME IN THE SEA

Whales are built for swimming. Their long, streamlined bodies let them slide through the water. Whales move their tails, called flukes, up and down to drive themselves along. They steer with their front **flippers**, which are like paddles. All whales have thick **layers** of fat, called blubber, under their skin. The blubber keeps them warm.

There are several dozen species, or kinds, of whales. These whales can be sorted into two groups. Toothed whales eat fish and **squid**. Baleen whales have strips called baleen instead of teeth. The whales use the baleen to **strain** food, such as tiny **plankton**, out of the water.

Baby whales are called calves. The mother and calf shown here are humpback whales. These whales spend the summer in the Arctic.

A WHALE'S LIFE

Most whales travel in groups, called pods. To stay in touch, whales talk to each other with different kinds of sounds. Whales squeak and groan. Some even sing. People think their low songs may help whales find **mates**.

After whales mate, it takes a whole year before a single baby is born. The newborn has to get up to the surface to breathe right away or it will drown. The baby nuzzles up to its mother, and she **squirts** milk into its mouth. A baby nurses for about a year. The mother and baby stay close together. Sometimes they pat each other with their flippers.

Bowhead whales can live for a very long time. Some bowheads may live as long as 200 years!

DEEP-DIVING BOWHEAD WHALES

Bowhead whales are the biggest whales that live in the Arctic year-round. These whales got their name because their heads are shaped like hunting bows. The bowhead's head is nearly half the length of its whole body! Bowheads are also known as Greenland right whales and Arctic whales.

Bowheads live in small pods in the cold Arctic waters. They have coats of blubber that may be 20 inches (51 cm) thick to keep them warm. Bowheads are baleen whales. They often strain small animals out of the upper waters. Other times, they dive deep to find food. Bowheads can dive down 500 feet (152 m).

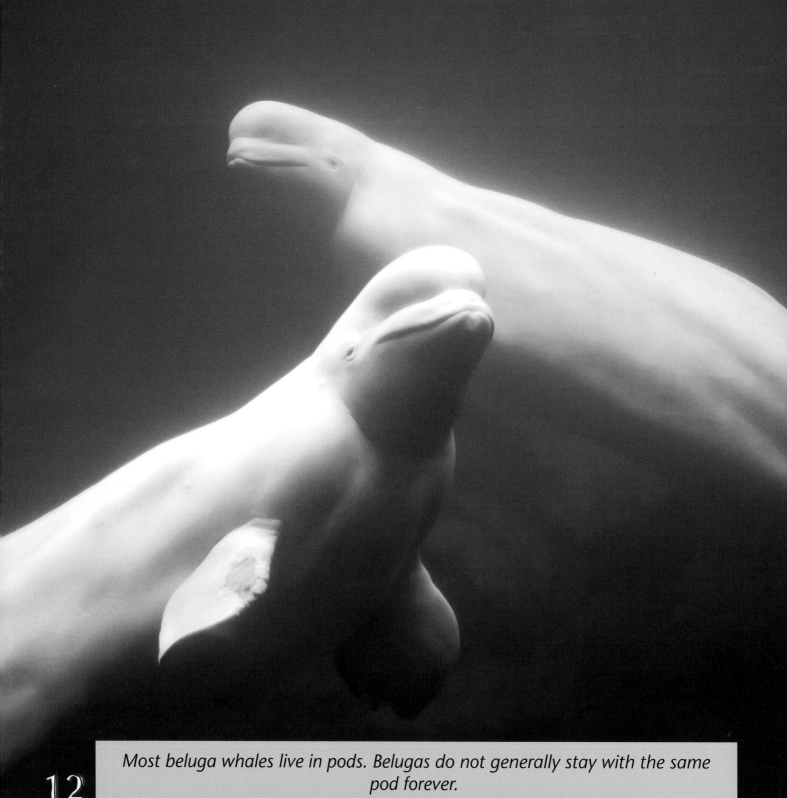

Most beluga whales live in pods. Belugas do not generally stay with the same pod forever.

BEAUTIFUL BELUGA WHALES

Belugas also live year-round in the Arctic. Like other Arctic whales, they have very thick layers of blubber. An adult beluga whale is bright white. No other whale is white all over. Some people call the beluga the white whale. Belugas are also known as sea canaries because of their songs. These whales squeal, click, and **whistle**. You can even hear their songs above water.

Beluga whales are also called squid hounds. While belugas do eat a lot of squid, they also eat fish, octopuses, worms, and whatever else they can find. They catch their food with their sharp teeth.

In the past, traders sold narwhal tusks, claiming that they were unicorn horns!

STRANGE-LOOKING NARWHALS

Narwhals are the oddest-looking Arctic whales. Each male narwhal has a very long tusk, or tooth, growing out of its upper **jaw**. The tooth spirals, or twists, out through the whale's upper lip. The tusk grows throughout a male narwhal's life. A narwhal's tusk can grow to be up to 10 feet (3 m) long. Narwhals are sometimes called unicorns of the sea because of their tusks.

What does a narwhal do with that giant tusk? Scientists are not sure, but some think that males use their tusks to fight each other to decide who gets to mate with females.

16 *Humpback whales often breach, or throw themselves high out of the water. They also lobtail, or hit their flukes against the water's surface.*

SINGING HUMPBACK WHALES

Humpback whales spend only part of the year in the Arctic. These baleen whales spend their summers feeding in the rich Arctic waters. The whales gulp down as much as 5,500 pounds (2,495 kg) of food every day. Each winter, humpbacks travel thousands of miles (km) to **tropical** waters, where they mate and have babies.

Humpbacks bend their backs into humps when they are ready to dive. This is how they got their name. Humpbacks are real **acrobats**. They often leap out of the water. Sometimes they spin around as they leap. Humpbacks are also known for their long, beautiful songs, which can last 20 minutes.

These blue whales are swimming past Vancouver Island, in Canada, on their way to the Arctic.

GRAY WHALES ON THE MOVE

Gray whales spend the summer in the Arctic waters, too. These whales are gray with white spots. Whalers, or whale hunters, once called gray whales devilfish because they would fight back wildly when they were caught.

All summer long, gray whales feed on the ocean floor, using their baleen to **sieve** through the mud for small animals. When winter is about to come, gray whales all swim south. They travel over 6,000 miles (9,656 km) all the way to the waters off Mexico. There, they mate and raise their young. During that time, the adult whales hardly eat at all. They live off their blubber.

This picture from the 1800s shows people whaling, or hunting, for bowhead whales in the Arctic.

WHALES AND PEOPLE

Whales have been important to Arctic people for thousands of years. The people of the Arctic eat whale blubber and meat. They use the baleen to make tools, baskets, and works of art. Whale bones are used to build houses and to make tool handles.

In the 1800s, other people, such as Europeans and Americans, started hunting Arctic whales. These people made whale oil from the whales' blubber, which they burned in lamps. They also used the whales' baleen to make fishing rods, umbrella ribs, and many other things. These whalers hunted so many whales that whales began to disappear from the oceans, and people became worried.

SAVING THE WHALES

In 1946, people from several countries got together to try to save the whales. These people made rules about how many whales could be hunted each year. In 1986, these countries put an almost total stop to whaling. The one exception is that the Arctic people still may hunt a few whales for oil and food.

There are fewer whales left than there were before whaling started, but many of these huge mammals are making a comeback. The gray whale is a real success story. There are now about 21,000 of them. That is at least as many as there were before whaling. There is hope for the whales!

GLOSSARY

acrobats (A-kruh-bats) Those who have good control of their bodies and can jump, flip over, and change positions quickly.

flippers (FLIH-perz) Wide, flat body parts that help animals swim.

jaw (JAH) Bones in the top and bottom of the mouth.

layers (LAY-erz) Thicknesses of something.

mates (MAYTS) Partners for making babies.

plankton (PLANK-ten) Plants and animals that drift with water currents.

sieve (SIV) To sort the parts of a mix by pouring out the water.

squid (SKWID) An animal with 10 legs that lives in the ocean.

squirts (SKWURTS) Pushes out in a thin stream.

strain (STRAYN) To sort out large pieces.

surface (SER-fes) The outside of anything.

tropical (TRAH-puh-kul) Warm year-round.

warm blooded (WORM BLUH-did) Having a body heat that stays the same, no matter how warm or cold the space around the body is.

whistle (HWIH-sul) To make a high, clear sound by blowing through the lips or teeth.

INDEX

A
acrobats, 17

B
babies, 5, 9, 17
baleen, 7, 21
blowholes, 5

F
fish, 5, 7, 13
flippers, 7, 9

J
jaw, 15

L
layers, 7, 13

M
mammals, 5, 22
mates, 9
milk, 5, 9

P
people, 5, 9, 13, 21–22
plankton, 7

S
squid, 7, 13

summer(s), 17, 19
surface, 5, 9

T
tops, 5

W
winter, 17, 19

WEB SITES

Due to the changing nature of Internet links, PowerKids Press has developed an online list of Web sites related to the subject of this book. This site is updated regularly. Please use this link to access the list: www.powerkidslinks.com/brrr/whales/